HowE

How

Smoking

Marijuana

Your Step By Step Guide To Quitting Weed

HowExpert with Michaela Wallace

For more tips related to this topic, visit HowExpert.com/quitmarijuana.

Recommended Resources

- HowExpert.com – Quick 'How To' Guides on All Topics from A to Z by Everyday Experts.
- HowExpert.com/free – Free HowExpert Email Newsletter.
- HowExpert.com/books – HowExpert Books
- HowExpert.com/courses – HowExpert Courses
- HowExpert.com/clothing – HowExpert Clothing
- HowExpert.com/membership – HowExpert Membership Site
- HowExpert.com/affiliates – HowExpert Affiliate Program
- HowExpert.com/writers – Write About Your #1 Passion/Knowledge/Expertise & Become a HowExpert Author.
- HowExpert.com/resources – Additional HowExpert Recommended Resources
- YouTube.com/HowExpert – Subscribe to HowExpert YouTube.
- Instagram.com/HowExpert – Follow HowExpert on Instagram.
- Facebook.com/HowExpert – Follow HowExpert on Facebook.

Table of Contents

Chapter 1: Introduction

Marijuana, commonly going by street names such as weed, pot, ganja, dope, grass, hemp, Mary Jane, reefer, Texas tea, bhang etc. is one of the easiest drugs that cause addiction. The user gains partial or total dependence on it. Without it, the consumer feels "not okay". One puff will lead to another and before you know, you are hooked.

We all have our reasons for depending on marijuana. We may need to boost our appetite; through the munchies it brings. We may need it before bedtime because it induces peaceful and sound sleep. We may need it to relax our minds whenever we are tense. We may need it to give us unyielding confidence to face certain situations bravely.

We may need to take marijuana to give us the motivation to do work or task assigned to us. Take for example, highness on pot for some people gives them the urge to dust and clean the whole house until it is sparky. That highness takes them closer to a sense of intense cleanliness. This is normal, until you get to a point you realize you cannot do anything without having to light up a joint or two.

We at times contemplate a lot on whether to go "clean" or not. Admit it, you've set yourself rules sometime and tried to "detox". Such are the terms you will find potheads using as they try to get rid of their addiction in coded language. Frankly, it is not easy to quit what you've been hooked on a long while.

We at times experiment on some things and before we know, it's too late to get out of. Too late is never too late though. Nothing is impossible with determination. This may sound far-fetched, but really it's not. The process may be a grueling one but it sure is going to be worth it at the end of the day.

The process to recovery is going to take some time, and this is why you may see parents taking their affected kids to rehab. Short for rehabilitation centers, many people opt for this because they won't have to do it by themselves but under the guidance of an institution. But even so, the same procedure is going to be required in the process too quitting. The only difference is, at home you will be doing it on your own, at your own pleasure and free will yet at the rehab, a guide will strictly take you through the process of renouncing the smoking.

The following eBook is here to take you through the process, encourage you to get through to the end and ultimately clean life that you desire. We humans are all different, we have acknowledged that fact in this case. That is why we have come up with several lists of the most befitting personal situations and experiences that might help you in getting rid of your addiction. Everyone has their way of dealing with situations and we have tried to come up with possible solutions for each and every one of you.

We sincerely hope it will help recovering addicts.

Chapter 2: Acceptance

What is Acceptance?

William Jones is known for his famous quote, "Be willing to have it so. Acceptance of what has happened is the first step to overcoming consequence of misfortune." Understanding what the problem of an issue in depth then accepting is the best way of handling it. It is human nature to want to be in control of situations and take charge of them. It is also human nature to fail to understand the situations we find ourselves in and accept them for what they are. Instead, we continue to live in denial, sticking to the same decisions we make, and failing to see what is really right.

Do not feel weird about severally telling yourself to quit but instead you find yourself having more than the usual. Wanting to quit but not being able to control the smoking process could be one of the major reasons for continued ingestion of marijuana. This is solely because we do not understand what we are going through at the moment. This is when you know you are addicted. The fact that you want to quit is positive for some reason though. It means you are ready to leave the habit and forge ahead for better.

Easy sounding yes? On the contrary, it is the opposite. The acceptance process is a long one, involving too. It needs a person to be completely honest with themselves or whoever their guide to recovery is. Hoping the guide is not the marijuana itself. On a light note there, because it happens. After all, didn't we seek solace in it sometime. A one more time couldn't hurt, is what we will tell ourselves right after that.

Are you ready to accept your addict behavior and release it for the maximum good? Well then, we can get to it right away.

How Addicted Am I?

Marijuana has an ingredient called THC, scientifically termed as delta9-tetrahydrocannabinol. It is an area of fascination and can cause serious addiction if not checked. If you are reading this now, you probably know by now how it works. Not really how it works, but how effective and addictive it can be. How powerful it can get, bringing forth the intoxication and psychoactive effects.

How will you know you are addicted to marijuana? It's quite simple. All you need to do is a self-assessment. Ask yourself these questions; how deep am I into the marijuana usage? How does your life function without marijuana? Would you like your marijuana usage to change?

Knowing the level you are at helps a great deal with the process. You need to know where you are before you decide on which way to go. Gauging intermittent usage is the way to go first. How much weed do you consume over a certain period of time? Perhaps, prepare a table where you put down your findings on the weekly, monthly or even daily, if it is that serious?

Keeping tracks of the smoking sessions can be hectic but you are required to take them in order to pass this first step. Also, the recollection process can be grueling but take your time. You can keep up with the marijuana usage as you record the times you take your pot for a while then get started once you are ready. Disclaimer, try not to take forever. In that case, this booklet will be of no use. And that is not what we expect of it.

We get addicted to the good things in life. This is why we easily get addicted to the "weed". As much as it has its share of side effects, weed is good in some aspects. Otherwise how else would you explain your addiction! We will want a slight or heavy effect it when doing certain things and this is undeniably true. But then, if you have also found your way to this article, you must be thinking hard about ways of quitting. You are in the right place.

What are the Benefits of Smoking Marijuana?

You will be surprised to know there are many benefits of ingesting marijuana. They may not necessarily manifest and we may not possibly notice them, but there certainly are benefits linked to its usage. They are as follows:

- Reduced anxiety
- Cancelling out the effects of tobacco carcinogens to improve the health of the lungs
- Helps ease acute pain
- Prevents cancer from progressing in some amounts
- Increases treatment effectiveness
- Aids in metabolism keeping your weight in check
- Increased levels of creativity
- In case of trauma or panic attacks the brain is offered protection from damage
- Elimination of nightmares
- Sound sleep effects
- Stimulation of appetite, popularly termed "Munchies"
- Counter effect for alcohol drinking addiction
- Reduced depression
- Good for diabetics
- Reduced epileptic seizures

Chapter 3: Do a Self-Background Check? Self-Vetting

What is Self-Vetting?

You may want to perform a personal check on yourself to know the extent of the addiction and put down the ways you think of will be helpful in the process. Know what you have been doing right. Similarly, know what you haven't been doing right. The moment we know where we have been going wrong it is easier to accept as we have discussed and leave it behind and stride ahead. This is roughly what is meant by self-vetting.

Have you been developing abnormal signs from smoking marijuana?

I Am Addicted

How much into it are you? Make a list of the things you feel it improves. Have a Y/N beside it. Y for yes, N for No.

- ✓ Does it help you sleep?
- ✓ Does it help you get your work done?
- ✓ Does it make experiences more pleasurable? So much you have to smoke it before you do anything?
- ✓ Does it help you relax?
- ✓ Does it help you unwind after a long day at work?

- ✓ Does it help you momentarily forget about your problems?
- ✓ Do you need it to bond with your friends?
- ✓ Do you need it to give you confidence outside the house or at social gatherings?
- ✓ Does it help you bond with your companion better? Do you need it to open up about some things? Does marijuana give you the courage to speak up about some things you otherwise wouldn't say when sober?
- ✓ Does it help you eat? How much appetite does marijuana give you?
- ✓ Does it help drive away sentiments you wouldn't love to have at that moment?
- ✓ Does it give your body a feeling you like?
- ✓ Is it a habit you just like doing? Is it your daily dose of "session"?
- ✓ Is it what you when idle?
- ✓ Do you always have to smoke it when with your clique?

Despite the fact that you have a long list of good and positive experiences with ingesting marijuana, there has to be the counter feeling.

Do you always think twice about and before smoking marijuana? If so, this next stage is to help you put down the second thoughts you have about it.

- ✓ All drugs are costly. How much is your expenditure on weed, over a certain period of time?
- ✓ How much do you spend on the food you take to heal your munchies?

- ✓ How much do you have to spend on the other activities instead of getting work done?
- ✓ Do you have piled up debts because of marijuana? Whether directly or indirectly?
- ✓ How slow does marijuana make you?
- ✓ Does weed make you anti-social?
- ✓ Do you have cases of pot-related paranoia?
- ✓ Do you hate your addiction? Do you feel bad that you take marijuana but yet you still find yourself taking more?
- ✓ Do you get slowed down under the influence?
- ✓ Do you get into family feuds? Has it affected your relationship with your family members? Are they worried about you and your addiction?
- ✓ If not mutual, does it affect your relationship with your spouse?
- ✓ Do you fear it will have an effect on your kids, if you are a parent?
- ✓ Weed is illegal. Do you know you risk getting arrested by the cops? Does the thought of serving jail time or community service scare you?
- ✓ Does weed make you unnecessarily exhausted most of the time?
- ✓ Do you have to conceal it from people? Do you feel ashamed about it? Do you keep away from people due to weed?
- ✓ Does it make you do imprudent things? Do you often make ill-advised decisions when under the influence?
- ✓ Does it make you lazy? Is it interfering with your studies? Is it meddling with your employment life?
- ✓ Are you tired of it? Is it becoming too repetitive for you? do you feel the need to do something else in place of it?

✓ Has your tolerance continued to build up over the years you've been smoking or ingesting marijuana?

These questions must have run through your mind at one point or another. Don't resist it. It is good to be honest with yourself if you are going to heal from your addiction. Carefully write the list down in form of answers, giving more details on how it affects you. It is wise not to leave out any of the effects so go on a self-meditation process. You will need time to sit down and evaluate yourself in depth. Take your time.

If you have thought about the above very keenly, you must be ready for this next step. Admit it, at some point, you have sat down and imagined how going clean is going to help you reform your life.

Here I will require you to think about your life once you have quit the weed. Imagine it all and then make a list of the positivity you will find. You can write down what you think is negative as well, so that with time it is dealt with.

✓ Are you looking forward to better healthier friendships? Away from the addiction life?
✓ Do you look forward to the more savings of money you will have after quitting?
✓ Will you get better feeling you don't have to hide anything from you family and friends?
✓ Do you look forward to your added weight? Better nutrition for your body? A healthier lifestyle?
✓ Do you look forward to doing your work better and excelling at it?

- ✓ Will it make you better at your parenting skills? Will you have more time to spend with your kids and spouse too?
- ✓ Will you have other things apart from the weed to look forward to?
- ✓ Will you be able to combat your insomnia without the drug?
- ✓ Will you embrace the new change of lifestyle? Focus on more positive things in life?
- ✓ Will you have a better memory of things?
- ✓ Will you have directed your rejuvenated vigor into better things?
- ✓ Will you be proud of yourself?

The above questions are important because as a drug addict you will need to see your life from a better perspective so that you can get the motivation to really quit ingesting the drugs. We are certain these questions will help you relate with your current situation. If not, I doubt you are ready for the "cleansing" process.

You will need to have investigated your life from every possible angle to get started on the journey to recovery. This book is here to help you achieve that easily. From personal experiences, the hurdle about drugs is not the starting part but the coping part. It will be easy to start, but once you are hooked on it, the hardest part will be leaving the drug life behind you.

You will need to be patient. Quitting doesn't just take a day or two or three, neither one year. Simply, it has no range of specific quit period. It will all depend on your motivation. It is hard work, toning down on a lifestyle you were so much into. This will require the aid of people close to us. You will need to relinquish your stoner friends, unfortunately, because most of the time, it is the company we have that lead us into such temptations.

I Want to Quit!

We have taken you through the self-checking you have to put yourself through. However, it is not enough. You will need to make another list of thoughts that will serve as the challenges you will experience along the way as you hope to recover from the marijuana addiction. I still insist on you being honest with yourself so that the process won't be very complicated for you.

What do you think will hinder you from quitting marijuana? Put it down as follows:

✓ Are you undergoing so many problems that will take a toll on you if you decide to cut down or quit smoking?
✓ Will your friends or clique be a hindrance?
✓ Will you find it hard to say no to weed if your friends offer you some?
✓ Are you worried that you will lose your "cool" friends?
✓ Will it be hard to deal with your problems?
✓ Do you feel you will have nothing to do once you quit the weed?
✓ Do you have weed cravings and scared you will not be able to control them?

- ✓ Are you worried about the emotional turmoil that will follow you once you quit smoking?
- ✓ Does your spouse still smoke and you feel tempted?
- ✓ Will you find it hard to unwind or relax without "hitting the blunt"? Yes, yes. I know that look.
- ✓ Are you afraid that you might become like people leading a normal life?
- ✓ How readily available is the weed? Is it easy to come by?
- ✓ Would you lack a means of channeling away your troubles momentarily?
- ✓ Will things stop seeming interesting?
- ✓ Would your outlook on life change?

To understand how deep you are into the drug, you need to know the extent to which it affects you. even the physiological details should be taken into consideration as they could be majorly affected.

The **Severity of Dependence Scale (SDS)** is the standard scale to which you can tell your level of dependence on the weed. A score of three plus is an indication that you are highly dependent on it. And the not so good news is that the larger the dependence, the tougher it will be to quit weed. But it does not really matter the score on the scale, you can always quit if you really want to.

SDS   score dependence rating

0-3   nil or negligible

4-6   mild

7-9	moderate
10-12	substantial
13-15	severe

With the above table scale, you can use to calculate your dependence. The questions we have gone through above will guide us to getting the right calculation.

Write down the multi-choice questions, with the answers being very difficult, impossible, quite difficult, or alternatively, never, sometimes, almost not, barely for time related questions.

You need to write down the calculations over a period of at least three months. Multiply the number of questions by the number of months. Then tally your findings against each of the questions' answers and the number they carry.

For easier work, we will have an illustration as follows:

1) *How much into it are you?*
A. Not so much addicted   0
B. Addicted   1
C. Controllable   2
D. Cannot do without it   3
2) *Do you have things that hinder you from quitting marijuana?*

A. A great deal   0
B. Quite a lot   1
C. A little   2
D. Avoidable   3

3) *Do you think your life will get better after quitting the weed?*
A. No   0
B. Difficult to say   1
C. Hard but possible   2
D. Yes   3

4) *Does your addiction bother you?*
A. Never or almost never   0
B. Sometimes   1
C. Often   2
D. Always or nearly always   3

5) *Are you ready to quit?*
A. No   0
B. Not sure   1
C. Gradually   2
D. Yes   3

You have an SDS score of -----/15. This indicates a ------ level of dependence.

Chapter 4: Personal Transformation

Now that we have done thorough background checks on the different aspects related to ingestion of marijuana, we can now go ahead and plan on the steps to recovery. The analysis we have done on our addiction lives is important in providing the necessary actions to take to ensure a recovery goes on to completion.

This process will require dedication from the affected party in order for realization of what we are looking to achieve. And that's the drug-free life. There will be numerous hurdles along the way but it's up to an individual to be willing to overcome them and forge ahead.

This whole process is a journey. And our destination is a clean life free from marijuana ingestion. That is why we are going to break down the recovery steps into sections that will get us there.

We are going to use Prochaska and DiClemente's research based solution which proved that human beings normally go through certain known stages that will help in the quest to change addiction and habits we've come to get used to.

Pre-Contemplation

At this stage you as the user try to meditate on your current life, while you try so hard to convince yourself that what you are doing is perfectly okay. You don't see it necessary to quit smoking marijuana and you're okay with it. You're probably thinking of all the possible ways to give yourself inner peace that you can live with what you're doing.

Contemplation

This is the point where your pre-contemplation has yielded some results. You are aware that you need to quit the addiction and possibly noticed that it is affecting your life more than you think. You're looking at the negative effects of the weed. Is it becoming too much expensive for You? Do you feel like you could use the money you spend on drugs elsewhere? Is it interfering with your health? Are you cutting weight so fast? Are you slugging at your work? Your partner may still want to go on with the habit yet you plan on quitting. These are the challenges that a person must deal with at this point.

Decision

Seems like our contemplation yielded something after all. At this point, you have come to the conclusion that the amounts of marijuana you've been ingesting are a threat to your health. And as your health is a priority, you will be required to cut down on the smoking until none is left. Make up your mind and hold the focus on. This is personal and care should be taken to make an achievable goal.

Action

This is the most important stage. Which involves really quitting the weed. You could also cut down on the smoking because continued cutting down could lead to complete quitting. Once you have started this, there is hope in the coming days.

Maintenance

Action alone is not enough. There will be daily temptations that you will face. You might be tempted to take more if you were cutting down on the intake. Similarly, you might be tempted to smoke a joint when you had quit. This will need a lot of patience and discipline. The company we hang with need to be able to support you in your decision. You need to be consistent with your new usage levels, a little or none at all.

Relapse

This happens if maintenance fails its part. You may find yourself having more than you were already using. And it even becomes harder to quit at this point. It happens when we lose hope in the journey and decide to back to our previous lifestyle. If you really want to complete the journey to recovery, you must not relapse.

It is important to note that these steps form a cycle that can be hard to abandon. You may find yourself repetitively stuck at the same position of continued usage. This is quite normal and you should not worry much about it.

Relapse happens to a lot of people. You may want to quit the weed but several reasons that you personally know are hindrances to your goals of quitting. Such that, you get comfortable with your usage.

You need to work hard at one stage to overcome the successive stages. This is the task at hand. That you have successfully cut down on your usage or quit completely. As your goals dictate.

Your Ingredients

Throughout the journey you will require the following:

Preparation

You will need to make several preparations that will get you ready for the journey. Imagine yourself going on a picnic. What do you need to have with you? In this case, we need to quit our drug addiction. What are we going to require? Go back to the lists we had made and look for your preferred requirements.

Effort

To get to the destination we will need to put in appreciable effort to see us through. Your hard work will determine how fast you get to achieve your goals. Diverse ways of implementation

It is not only one way, the mentioned way that is going to help you quit your addiction. You will need a number of means to get there. Write down all the possible ways that could help you out and try to see which is easy to follow and go with that. We want to do this with as much comfort as we can get.

Set clear goals

You need to know what you are really after and make your mind on it. If you want to quit completely, know that is your goal. They should be as precise and to the point. This doesn't give any room for confusion.

Future planning

Truth is, if you picture yourself at a certain point in life, you are likely to get there as your dreams become more real. Plan on your future goals and you will get there easily.

Strategies

You must put in place strategies that will help you achieve your goals. These will help us in undertaking the plans we have lined up.

Creativity

There are many ways we will have to implement in the process to recovery. You will need to be creative with your plans, improving further on the ones you have set to yield better performance. For example, if you used to take marijuana as a reason to get rid of stress, you will need to come up with other means of managing the stresses that will hit you.

Plans to Make Changes

- Write down a list of things you plan on achieving. The following are examples:
- I want to Quit smoking
- I want to cut down on my marijuana usage
- I want to smoke with healthier means such as using vaporizers or bongs
- I want to smoke only before I sleep
- I want to smoke after work
- Write down your goal if it has not been provided in the above list.

Users should be warned that getting out of an addiction requires a lot of patience and determination. It is difficult to get out of such a habit and you will require distractions to help you replace your old habits and embrace the new ones.

What will be your replacement strategy for the times you will decide to quit?

- I will go on about reading books
- I will go hang out with my non-smoker friends
- I will go to the gym/workout
- I will write a blog; I will do some articles.
- I will go help out at a community service center

Implementation of Change

We are started now.

Withdrawals

There are certain psychological and physical symptoms that will come up as a result of the cutting down or quitting process. These are what we refer to as withdrawals. The psychological ones are the most difficult to deal with. They pose a lesser danger as compared to their physical counterparts.

Such symptoms include restlessness, being fidgety, moments of confusion, increased levels of anxiety, the strong urges to smoke up, depression and blank stares into nothing.

Physical symptoms may include instances of diarrhea, throwing up (vomiting), loss of sleep, nightmares, sweating at night, mild fevers and restlessness.

If you are experiencing these, you should be happy. These are an indication that the body is reacting to the new changes in habits. They are good signs of recovery.

The good thing about withdrawals is they don't last too long. If you are serious about really quitting, it could take you approximately one to two weeks, three at most to get over the withdrawals.

Physical dependence on marijuana is rare and as much as the first few days of recovery are hectic; it is relatively easy to get through. You may fail to notice the difference between withdrawals and your usual moods. This is a norm.

How can you cope with withdrawals?

o   *Self-care* – this is the time you need to give yourself maximum concentration. Focus on yourself. Your health too. Eat well, a balanced diet, stay healthy, eat lots of fruits, workout as much as you can. Get rid of the extra steam you need to release.

o   *Patience* – You will need constant patience, for about two to three weeks, or more, if you were hooked entirely. The tough times will pass in no time.

o   *Less stimulants* – try to avoid caffeinated drinks such as tea, coffee or other stimulants such as nicotine containing substances like cigarettes. This will cause insomnia. And we are trying to sleep as much as we need to get rid of the addiction.

o   *Let your people know* – It is wise to let the people you spend a lot of time with that you are cutting down or quitting your weed intake so that they can support you. They will sail you through just fine. They will also understand if you develop unusual mood swings.

o   *Old is gold* – Since time immemorial warm baths have been known to be sleep inducers as well as magical relaxers. In case you are thinking of hitting the blunt again, try to treat yourself to such and you will be surprised. We need to keep you as active and occupied as possible to prevent the possibility of a relapse.

Keep track of your withdrawals in the following table. Write your entries for the new day daily.

DAY 1	MILD	MODERATE	ACUTE
Anxiety			
Restlessness			
Cravings			
Insomnia			
Night sweats			
Lost concentration			
Headaches			
Poor appetite			

Tick wherever applicable. Make the records daily for up to one-month period.

Manage Your Urges

An urge, commonly going by the name cravings, is a term used to describe a short-lasting feeling that comes up when you desire to have a drug in your body system. It is part of the recovery process and you shouldn't feel odd about it.

The challenge here is how to keep these cravings away to ensure your recovery process goes through successfully. They are one of the top reasons for a relapse. They are usually accompanied by restlessness and agitated feelings. These need to be kept in check.

Or else one might find themselves back to the smoking zone to satisfy your craving.

It could be the most stressful thing you'd have to deal with. You need to hang in there a little longer to get past it. You will be pleased to know these urges lessen with time and you'll soon be leading a pot-free life. You need positive motivation and this you can get from a lot of places as we are going to see.

As we have seen, addiction can be a pain in the ass. Changing habits even worse. Since the victim's body expects to ingest a certain amount of the THC at certain times of the day, it is normal to want again, despite trying to control your intake.

Urge surfing, a condition where the cravings come and go in patterns like waves, is quite rampant amongst heavy users of the drug. Your resistance to the drug increases with reduction in the number of cravings you experience.

There are ways that have been known to work for most people and I'm sure picking a number of your favorite actions from them will help a great deal. As follows:

- *Personal study* – you need to keep regular tabs on yourself, carefully, to know when the cravings kick in. This will aid in monitoring your conditions easily.
- *Build your resistance* – gradual control of your cravings leads to easy management. You need to

ensure maximum resistance so that you can reap as much from it.

- *Distractions* – do anything else to keep you away from temptations to smoke. It is advisable that you occupy yourself in what you will enjoy doing. You could watch your favorite show, go play soccer or some football, cooking for others. Etc.
- *Workout* – workouts are a positive way to let off the negative steam your body is harboring. This is a healthy means to keep off cravings as much as it is good for your body.
- *Set achievable goals* – using the delaying tactic, you can keep postponing the time you have set to smoke. This could lead to an improved body resistance to the drug.
- *Helpful company* – as much as you have company, try to get a supportive company. Surround yourself with people who understand you and are willing to help you through the process.
- *Avoid your weed buddies* – peer is another influence. You may need to avoid friends from your past if you are to keep clean. Hanging around people who are smoking can be tempting and you could easily lose your control here.
- Warm baths
- Go to a massage parlor get yourself some rejuvenating tissue kneading.
- *Get a mentor* - Talk to recovering addicts. A share of your story might just be your way out. Such people provide the inspiration to quit.
- Indulge in physical exercises, take your dog for a run, stroll or ride a bike.
- Treat yourself – every milestone requires some sort of appreciation. This is because each will leave

you stronger. You need to reward your progressive self and watch more motivation coming your way.

Cutting Down

Diversity is the spice of life. What may comfortably work for you may not work for another. You need to be flexible in whatever means you use to recover. You need to try all the possible ways to curb it because taking too long may just be hectic and cause one to give up. You will find some have given up and so they just smoke up to keep up with their lost control. This shouldn't be the case.

We need to take control of our emotions. This way we are able to handle every different situation that comes our way. We need strong will to be able to cut down on the weed consumption because it needs effort.

There are different means we could use to ingest the weed. Some are advisable, some not. The following ways could help cut down our cannabis intake:

- *Hail leaf butter* – did you know baked weed products such as weed cookies, weed chocolates, weed cakes and even weed simsim. These regulate our intake. They take some time to take effect and also last a long while in our bodies. Hence, for less consumption, the same effect is achieved.
- *Joints instead of bongs* – it is healthier to use joints. A good feeling that lasts long, then you will not be able to roll another joint because you are

already too baked. It also poses a lesser risk for lung diseases.

- *Spend less on weed* – Try to substitute your drug budget with better things. You could get yourself one of those watches, or whatever you'd like, and concentrate on the new feeling. This way you can handle your expenses. They may be cheaper in bulk, but you may end up smoking all of it before the time it's supposed to last.
- *Vaporizers* – breathing in the burning smoke is unhealthy for the lungs. This is the downside of smoking up. However, a vaporizer heats up the THC element in the weed enough to be produced smoke-free. This is good for your lungs.

Chapter 5: With Change Comes Replacement

People are different and you will find that everyone has their way of getting over their addictions. Some people prefer to go the "cold turkey" way i.e. they decide once and for all to quit and they don't do the weed anymore. This has been found to be the most effective.

The downside of telling yourself to cut down on the weed gradually with time is that it takes time and one may end up taking more than they had anticipated. Since it also takes time, relapse occurs at higher chance here. It's always advisable to make a stern decision to quit marijuana and stay clean for good, if you really want to quit.

However, depending on the method you choose, you will need strategies to keep you in place. We have discussed below.

Relaxation Methods

A large percentage of pot users consume it for relaxation purposes. If the quitting process has to be effective, this needs to be taken care of. Once we eliminate the root cause or find alternatives for it, we can then go ahead and tackle the main issue at hand.

Do you just get bored and decide to light a joint up? how often do you get bored? Is weed the first thing you think of when you find yourself bored? Do you think it is healthy? Are you worried about it? These are the questions that are definitely running through your mind when we are talking about boredom for marijuana addicts.

Do not be ashamed about the condition. It is normal to try out substances that make us feel high. We should embrace our conditions and the fact that they need our attention. Then we will be able to find remedy for ourselves. This is a process that requires consistence and support. We are advised to bring our best of behaviors along.

So, back to relaxation. How else can you relax? How else can you take your mind off those things you don't want to think of? Fact is, smoking up isn't going to solve our problem but create dependence. It may temporarily do, give you that good feeling, which I like to call an illusion, but then in the end, the same boredom is going to recur if we don't find alternative means to get out of our situations.

Means of relaxation

➢ *Hobbies* – we all got pastimes that make us feel good, with the least of efforts. These are what we need here in place of the weed. The following are examples of amusements:

- *Playing soccer* or football, soft ball, tennis, rugby. Pick a game you are good at and spend more of your time with it.
- *Knitting* clothes and fabrics.
- *Making designs* of stuff such as art, fashion or even drawings of various equipment from simulators. This is especially suitable for techie addicts.
- *Writing blogs* and related articles. Did you know that writing can be addictive if you just let your mind wander away for a considerable amount of time? In no time you might find yourself hoked. Necessary addictions so we say.
- *Watching shows* or movies from your favorite cable networks. Grab a new animation every day and try to watch it till the finish.
- *Cooking* – preparing food can be time consuming and addictive as well. Today you cook this, tomorrow you will want to make a better version of it. You try spice-free today tomorrow you spice it all over. You will realize a new form of indulgence. As much as it is fun to cook when stoned, especially looking forward to dissolve the munchies, it is barely healthy. This is because the metabolism rates caused by THC are so massive. They can get to even five times the normal rates. You will be forced to fill up your body with unnecessary foods that would not be beneficial.
- *Go hiking* – there are several hike spots in nature and it would be fun to go hiking instead of blazing indoors. Besides keeping the marijuana at bay, it will keep our bodies occupied and steaming off the extra energy we reserve in our bodies.
- *Learn* – there is so much knowledge out there. Now that we have an increasingly high number of

eBooks in the stores, such as Goodreads or Kindle, you can opt to read articles as you garner all the knowledge you can from it. This way our minds are occupied.

➢ *Farming activities* – do you have a firm or cabin in the wild? At the upcountry side? You can indulge yourself in farm activities such as ploughing wheat, or whatever crop you have grown. Spend more time with the animals. You will actually find some fun there and get over your boredom.

➢ *Workout* – doing exercises leaves the body feeling fresh. This is because endorphins are released in the process, leaving you feeling fit and good.

➢ *Yoga* – you think this is for hippies alone? Try it. The mental, physical and spiritual practices are a good way of meditation and improving on self-consciousness. With these, you can take easy control of your mind and body.

➢ *Laughter is the best medicine* – treat yourself to shows, stand-up comedies, stay around funny people so that you can enjoy their company and not think about the weed.

➢ *Let your muscles relax*- if our body muscles are feeling relaxed we tend to be at peace. Uncomfortable positions give rise to restlessness which may be bad for you, causing unease and finally you may think of hitting the blunt. Tense and relax the different parts of your body, each at a go so that you can attain maximum peace.

➢ *Engage yourself in fun activities* every other time so that there is no room for boredom. We know what boredom does to us. Try and hang out with new people, know their ways of life, try out their activities, you may find them more fun than you thought.

Write down your list of activities that could help you relax.

1.

2.

3.

4.

5.

6.

7.

De-Stressing

Feelings are much like waves; we can't stop them from coming but we can choose which one to surf. Daily as humans we undergo experiences that tend to upset our balance of emotions, be it euphoria or sadness.

We barely have any control over them. However, we can choose to let them break us or build us. We should take on the positive means. Pain can be excruciating and you may want to get away from it as soon as possible. This is why people resort to the blunt.

We know it feels like an instant relief once we smoke up but trust me, it is an addiction you would not love to create. Subsequent dependence on weed for stress removal can be the hardest to get over as daily life knocks us down. At times they may be overwhelming and you may be tempted to go overboard and do more drugs.

There are methods that can help you deal your stress. They may be quite similar to the means of relaxation, but now that it is an aftereffect of an issue, we need to handle it more differently.

➢ *Straight thinking* – circumstances or terrible news may throw us out of balance and shape and we may be seeking an instant way of trying to forget them so we hit the blunt. However, the first thing you should do is try and think straight. Take control of yourself. Know what you want and what you don't want. We blame the world for our misfortunes, curse, and possibly hurl all kinds of insults. This will lead us to a place where it would not be easy to get back from.

➢ *Know your emotions* – study your body and its reactions. Know what feeling to expect when something happens and be comfortable with it. accept it. Understand that it is part of you and what you are going through is normal. Accept them. Once you learn what to expect, you won't be outrageous and end up slipping back into the drug.

➢ *Don't give in just yet* – motivate yourself. Despite how hard the situation may be, don't throw in the towel. Learn to pass over these daily life hurdles by overcoming them. In the end you will stronger. You will feel better about yourself. As humans the sound of progress gives us good feelings and we become more proud of ourselves.

➢ *Realism* – we need to understand the fact that we cannot change some things. We cannot make people be who we want them to be. We cannot control what they do, the decision will always be theirs. Don't let other people be an influence on you. Don't decide to smoke to deal with the stresses other people bring upon you. Be wise. Make the right decisions.

➢ *Relaxation* – here we are again. See, all these are correlated. Despite the pressures we are under, we need to try and teach ourselves to relax. This way we won't face the temptations of having to smoke up to relieve ourselves of them.

Sleep Better

Do you face insomnia? Do you have trouble sleeping at night? Do you decide to hit the blunt before bedtime so you can get better sleep? You know do you. We are here to make you get rid of that. So that you will have normal sleeping patterns.

The following ways may help you sleep better:

➢ *Sleep diary* – you need to make a comparison between your daily life activities and sleep patterns to determine which practices make you sleep better. If you keep track of your sleep patterns for say two weeks you will develop a good habit that you will find it easy to sleep.

> *Avoid nicotine* – nicotine is a stimulant as we know and it is a hindrance to your sleep. Withdrawal pangs may cause night restlessness which will lead to you not getting a good night's sleep, if not none at all.

> *Exercise* – cardio-related workouts have been known to improve sleep quality and length. However, you should exercise at least 4 hours before bedtime. Try out the yoga stretches too.

> *Avoid caffeinated drinks before bedtime* – tea, cola, coffee contain caffeine which may last up to 8 hours in our bodies and may inhibit the brain from having any sleep.

> *Winding-down* – Dr. Breuss tells us "Sleep is not an on-off switch. It is more like easing your foot off the gas". After a hard day's work, you need to tone down and relax, give your body the time to transition and in the process the sleep will come easily. Plan for the following day's activities so you will know how much you need to sleep.

> *Sleep inducements* – you may decide to opt for a spray that has a sleep inducing effect before bedtime. Though the least advisable, you may pop a sleeping pill, with a prescription from your doctor, so that you don't find yourself hooked while we are trying to replace another drug addiction in the process.

Chapter 6: How to Prevent Chances of a Relapse

What is a Relapse?

Trying to abstain is not enough, because in the process, you may find yourself back to where you started all over again, using even more of the drug. This sudden return to the use of a drug is what we term as a **relapse**. It is normal for people who are trying to get over an addiction to have relapses along the way.

It is recommended as much as possible not to have a relapse because it is more dangerous than the addiction. For instance, you would feel the urge to continue using the drug, consume it in even larger amounts and then you would want to go to treatment and get done with it within the shortest time possible and this would be a big issue.

Every time you relapse, you learn something new about your addiction. It is not the best of feelings and one feels quite insufficient about themselves. It is a great deal to people who are recovering and that is why you will need to come along with your best behavior to get rid of your addiction.

Let's Find Distractions For You!

Hang out

There are so many joints to hang out and forget about drugs. You won't need drugs to enjoy. Live life. Be free. Take your time, go to cinemas, watch movies, sample the upcoming trailers and make it a habit. You will find them fun. Sample out new joints that come up around your place. Go to events that don't require you to use drugs to have fun. Go to fairs. Learn as much as you can.

Become active

Keeping yourself active is another possible way to easily get out of your drug addiction. When our bodies are lazy and idle, that is when we give room for thoughts of drugs, marijuana especially in this case. You can become active by becoming a member of a club. There are different kinds of clubs. Choose according to your passion. You may go to a sports club, join a book club, become a member of the poetry club. And so on.

Vacation

Holidays are one way to relax and give ourselves a fresh new start from everything. Going on a vacation would be a good way to feel good about yourself. In the process, you will end up feeling motivated and wanting to change so many aspects of your life, in this case the drug addiction. Treat yourself sometime, take yourself to a place you have always wanted to go.

Pamper yourself

You may be tired of the old life and would like some new spark to get rid of the old addictive drug life. Give yourself a makeover. Treat yourself to some good clothes shopping. Change your entire look. You will feel good about yourself and won't see the need to use the drugs. This will be part of a bigger change that we are looking to achieve.

Utilize your brain

An idle mind is the devil's workshop; the common saying goes. Well this is true, to some point. What do we do when we are idle? We make bad decisions. That's what mostly happens. To avoid being idle, and its subsequent temptations, we need to make good use of our brains. Grab a book, read on it. Watch an educative documentary. Do some art if you like to draw. Produce designs of everything you can think of, depending on your area of interest. Believe you me, you will forget the drug addiction.

Sense of touch

As humans we are sensitive to touch and touch makes us feel good or irritable. If you were smoking marijuana to help you not think about the activities you were indulging in, it is time to stop those activities. Go on, do what you love doing. You won't need a drug as a motivation. Learn to make love soberly with your partner, kiss, embrace and cuddle away all your weed desires. After all, isn't life all about being happy.

Good company

We might have smoked weed to look cool and to be able to relate with members of a certain group. You will need to avoid this company if you are to recover from the addiction. Learn not to give shoddy excuses. Be straight up about your motives. Tell them you are avoiding them because you don't want to be dragged back. You are recovering. Good company is good for you. coupled with the activities we have looked at; you will find better company that will keep you satisfied.

Nature

Nature is the most beautiful thing to happen to us on this earth. Insights and inspirations tell us that looking at the beauty of the world is the first step towards purifying the mind. It is the purest feeling the soul can experience. Going on nature trails, visiting parks, planting trees and flowers and other environmental activities leave you feeling good about yourself and the world. This perception will help us heal.

Take good care of your body

We may feel the need to smoke and ingest marijuana because we are not feeling good about our bodies. We smoke to be reckless. We cannot handle the feeling that we are sober and shaggy so we decide to use drugs. You know what would change this? You! None but you. learn to take good care of your body. Give it a proper bath, put on makeup if you may, good clothes and even good shoes and you will feel good. Take good care of your hair too.

Pleasure

So many activities in this world give us pleasure. Using drugs apparently is one on the list. It is unhealthy. We need to find activities that are effortlessly pleasing to us so we won't need a drug to make it better. It will be better by itself. Listen to good music, go about, sing and dance to them. You will find that in no time, you will have the pleasure.

Long Term Goals

These long term goals are just but an extension of what we have discussed above. You will need discipline to get through this. Recovery is not a one-time thing. It is a lifelong effort. It requires dedication and zeal. It requires you to have made a stern decision about quitting it and be focused on it.

We have seen the side effects of marijuana and the pain it brings. Despite feeling good momentarily, the long term effects are adverse. We need to take control of our lives and see the way forward to this drug-free life. It is easy, if we keep ourselves occupied and satisfied.

There is so much more you want from life and you know it. How will you go about it? ask yourself the following questions:

- o What are my areas of strength?
- o What are the things I love doing?
- o Which are the virtues I treasure? How will these values help me in my life?
- o How do I picture my future life?
- o What things can I do so well? Should people be a hindrance to your goals? They shouldn't matter. Only you should.

Chapter 7: Embracing the New Pot-Free Life

You are probably three to four to six weeks free of the marijuana and all you need to do is keep up. You are definitely feeling good about yourself. You are ready to take up on new challenges now that you have beat the drug addiction for one. Your life suddenly feels better. Anything can come your way and you will be sure to deal with it in the best possible means.

Brace Yourself

As much as we may be free of the influence, there will always be temptations that are out to get us to smoking again. Waves of life can also be so hard on us despite the many efforts we try to put into making our lives better. Life knocks us hard so many times, and for some it might go well, as expected, but others will keep facing the problems that they have always wanted to avoid.

The moment you know how you plan to cope with a certain situation once it arises, it is easier to evade the risks once they resurface. The risk times will always be there. It is like they are hunting you down. But being able to stand firm against the temptations will help a great deal. Know what you want. And you don't want a relapse. No now. You have come a long way to go back to where you started.

There are guidelines that will help you deal with your situation in case of risk times:

- You can go talk out your issues with a supportive person, one who understands you. Normally in this case family is a great deal.
- Therapy – going to a shrink has been known to help very many people who are battling issues within themselves. The counsellors provide the necessary insights, and alternative ways of coping with the issues.
- Go to meetings – sessions from people who are recovering are very inspiring. They help you realize that you are not alone and that you can maintain your healthy state for as long as you keep by the rules.
- If you have the option of discarding the situation, leave as you can. Don't let it eat you up.
- Use your past to build your future. If you were able to resist the urges and cravings back then, you definitely can right now as well.
- Try to remind yourself of the reasons why you had to quit. Look at the positive things you have done to yourself since you quit the weed. You will see that you have been doing well and that you need to keep up with it.

Consistence Is Key

By now you will have gained a whole new outlook on life since you began your abstinence. The renewed energy, the enthusiasm and all is a motivation to keep forging ahead. The biggest problem is consistency. Try and maintain the drug free life, for as long as you can.

At the end of every week or two of success, review your progress. Write down the positive aspects and the challenges as well. Don't put your expectations too high. This is a life process. It is going to take you a while to balance all the sides, but even so, life will be waiting for us with its challenges and it is up to us to take control of our lives and steer them in the direction we wish to go.

We had talked about self-monitoring. This is a big aspect in making changes to your life. After the rapid changes, you know you have to treat yourself for the hard work. Reward yourself as often as you can to give room for better growth.

Go about the activities we have talked about to ensure all is going well.

If you happen to relapse, try to take even more stern measures. Go back to the drawing table see where you went wrong. Write down the temptations. E.g. went to Harry's house, got stoned. Then go ahead and write how to avoid the situation. E.g. Don't go to Harry's house.

Go back through this workbook and try to see where you might have gone wrong.

What next? Diary? To-Do-List?

Put down a self-monitoring dairy. Make a customized one. Let it fit your needs.

Let your life be free. Now you are good to go. You don't need marijuana in your life anymore. Everything is all better. Read about people who have changed their lives after quitting. Motivation and inspiration stories will give you life. They will keep you focused. Tell you that life is more and you can do more for yourself.

At this point you will have made drastic improvements in your class work, employment life, sports and even personally. You are able to deal with your emotions better. More appropriately. You are able to pay your bills on time. Your priorities are well set. This is a good sign.

We sincerely hope this book will help you in overcoming your addiction problem. All the best.

Regards.

About the Expert

Michaela Wallace is a Maryland based writer who has watched her friends and family members get messed up by drugs, specifically marijuana. She has grown up living with them and therefore knows much about how it feels being an addict and not being able to quit. The experience she has written is personal and will take you through real life examples.

The book will be of great help to users who are out to reform their lives and serious about it. Michaela has also watched her brothers get over their addictions in triumph and this is why she has written this to tell the affected out there that it is possible to quit your addiction. It doesn't matter how deep you are into it, because it is possible to recover from it.

HowExpert publishes quick 'how to' guides on all topics from A to Z by everyday experts. Visit HowExpert.com to learn more.

Recommended Resources

- HowExpert.com – Quick 'How To' Guides on All Topics from A to Z by Everyday Experts.
- HowExpert.com/free – Free HowExpert Email Newsletter.
- HowExpert.com/books – HowExpert Books
- HowExpert.com/courses – HowExpert Courses
- HowExpert.com/clothing – HowExpert Clothing
- HowExpert.com/membership – HowExpert Membership Site
- HowExpert.com/affiliates – HowExpert Affiliate Program
- HowExpert.com/writers – Write About Your #1 Passion/Knowledge/Expertise & Become a HowExpert Author.
- HowExpert.com/resources – Additional HowExpert Recommended Resources
- YouTube.com/HowExpert – Subscribe to HowExpert YouTube.
- Instagram.com/HowExpert – Follow HowExpert on Instagram.
- Facebook.com/HowExpert – Follow HowExpert on Facebook.

Printed in Great Britain
by Amazon